EARLY QUAKER RECORDS

IN VIRGINIA

D1521714

Compiled By

MILES WHITE, JR.

REPRINTED WITH A NEW INDEX
By Anita Comtois

Baltimore
GENEALOGICAL PUBLISHING CO., INC.
1985

Excerpted and reprinted from
Publications of the Southern History Association,
Vol. VI (May 1902) - Vol. VII (May 1903)
With a new Index
Genealogical Publishing Co., Inc.
Baltimore, 1977, 1979, 1985
Copyright © 1977
Genealogical Publishing Co., Inc.
Baltimore, Maryland
Library of Congress Catalogue Card Number 76-46154
International Standard Book Number 0-8063-0745-5
Made in the United States of America

Publisher's Note

Abstracts based on the very records of which this work is issue, the so-called Chuckatuck Record, have been published in Volume VI of William Wade Hinshaw's *Encyclopedia of American Quaker Genealogy,* to which the reader is directed for a full account of the records, believed to be the oldest Quaker records in Virginia.

Genealogical Publishing Co., Inc.

EARLY QUAKER RECORDS IN VIRGINIA.

[The Association is indebted to Mr. Miles White, Jr., of Baltimore, Md., for this material. Brackets [ ] with enclosures have been inserted by him.
The following description has been furnished also through his efforts:
"Among the original records belonging to Baltimore Yearly Meeting of Friends, of which I am custodian, none is more frequently consulted than the book containing the earliest records of Friends in Nansemond and Isle of Wight counties, Va. This is probably largely due to the fact that Nansemond county was in early days largely peopled by the Puritan and the Quaker, and that the court and land records of this county were years ago destroyed by fire, and therefore any genealogical data relating to its residents is now eagerly sought after.

"Numerous pages have been in whole or in part cut out and doubtless much valuable material has thereby been lost, some entries are almost illegible and through constant use this old book has become so worn that it cannot last much longer if continually used, and therefore with the permission of the meeting, I have had the genealogical matter contained therein copied, and through the courtesy of these PUBLICATIONS now present the same to the public.

"The original spelling of all names and places has been carefully preserved and it will be noticed that the same name is often spelled differently in different entries.

"In Hotten's *List* will be found mention of various early Virginia settlers of the same names as those recorded herein, and in Neill's *Virginia Carolorum* mention is made of several of the persons spoken of herein, some of whom held office under the Colonial Government. Dr. Stephen B. Weeks frequently consulted this book while preparing his *Southern Quakers and Slavery*, in which accounts of some of these Friends are given, and in which also reference is made to other entries than those relating to genealogical matters. These other entries are probably of little general interest outside the Society of Friends and will not be given herein. They consist mostly of various letters from George Fox and from sundry meetings in England to Friends in Virginia: rules for the government of the meetings; communications from Isaac Pennington, John Cook, Edward Perkins, Richard Robinson, Joseph Glaister and other Friends; acknowledgments by various members of infractions of the rules of the Society; lists of Friends' sufferings, and settlement of boundaries and other questions at issue between members.

"The entries in the book begin at both ends, the marriages being mostly in one part and the births and deaths in the other, though some of each are found amongst the other class. The entries contained in the part principally devoted to marriages are given in this article, and those contained in the other part will be

1

given in subsequent ones. Though begun in 1673, the book contains some few entries relating to events that occurred at earlier dates, and which were doubtless recorded in pursuance of some action of the meeting, the minutes of which unfortunately have not been preserved.

"In addition to the genealogical data, I have given the opening entry in the book, and the form of marriage certificate spoken of by George Fox in a letter "sent from Elizabeth river to Friends at Nansemond in the 10th month 1672," in which he directed them "to keepe a mans meeting once a quarter," and gave instructions about it. The marriages of which digests are given herein, are recorded in the same, or nearly similar forms."—John C. Thomas.]

"This booke begun in the yeare 1763 by the motion & order of George ffox the servant of God.—Whearein is a register of th Nativitty of freinds Children according as their parents did give in in wrighting.—heare is allso to register all freinds Children that shall be borne hearafter and allso all Marriages & burialls that shall heare after happen amongst them."

Form of Marriage Certificate.

This "Certifycat is customary amongst ffreinds in all places in cases of Marriage."

"This is to certefy the truth to all people that A. B. of Lon: son of R. S. and C. D. of Bris: daughter of J. S. haveing intentions of mariage according to the ordenance of God & his Joyning did Lay it before the men & weomans meeting, before whom their Mariage was propounded, & then the meeting desired them to waight for a time, and so they enquireing betwixt the time wheather the man was free from all other weomen, and shee free from all other men, so the second time they comeing before the man & weomans meeting, all things being cleare, a meeting of the people of God was appointed for that purpose, wheare they tooke one another in the house of W. L. and in the presence of God & in the presence of us his people according to the Law of God & the practis of the holly men of God in the scriptures of truth and they theare promising before God & us his people to live faithfully togeather man &

wife as longe as they live, according to Gods honorable Mariage, they theare setting both their hands unto it the day of ――― in the yeare―――.

and wee are wittneses of the same whose names are heareunto subscribed."

RECORDS.

Margaret Tabbarer states in a paper sent to the meeting [probably in the 11th mo. 1768] that her daughter [name not mentioned] had been married to a young man [name not mentioned] by a Priest, and expresses her sorrow that she was married that way.

Tho: Hollowell and Alic his wife desire that their testimony be recorded against their childrens [names not mentioned] unlawful behavior in being married by Priests.

John Collings & Mary Tooke of ye county of Surry propounded their marriage before a meeting of Men & women frends at the house of william Bressies in ye County of Isleaweight one ye forth day of ye Eleventh month Last And at a meeting at Tho. Jordans in Chuckatuck in ye county of Nanzemund they did pubblish their marriage againe on ye eighth day of the twelfe month following and were married in the house of John Barnes hir father-in-law on the fourteenth day of ye twelfe month, 1682.

John Collings,
Mary Tooke.

Witnesses:	Saml Newton
John Barnes	Andrew Brown
Walter Barklett	Will. Hancock
Robt. Lace	Denis Reathdon
John Shepard	Mary Lacie
Edward Pancoast	Jane Barnes
James Johnstone	Alice Bartlett
William Goodman	Barbery Hooles
Edward Tanner	Ann Seward

Alice Shepard   Jane Tannar
Catheren Ronell   Eliz. Hancoke
Letes Lancaster   Rebecka Goodman

Robart Jones & Martha Rice of the county of Nanzemun propounded their marriage before a meeting of menn & women frends at Henry Wiggses howse in the county of the Isleaweight on ye seventh day of the fourth month last and coming before a meeting the second time at Elizabeth Bellsons howse in ye county of Nanzemun on ye fift day of this Instant month they did pubblish their marriage a second time and were married in his one howse on the tenth day of ye fift month in the year 1683

Robart Jones
Martha Rice

Witnesses: Francs Mace
Robart Lawrence Henry Hall
Thomas Jordan   Daniell Stamper
Edward Perkins   David Rice
Thomas Hollowell James Sumner
John Small   James Laseter
Will Sanders   John Rice
Tho. Page   Alce Hollowell
Will Newby   Mary Sanders
Tho. Duke   Margret Duke
Edmond Belson   Eliz. Hall.

On the 11 day of the 7 Mo 1700 wee understand there is in the Costidy of Margerett Jordan the elder widdow to say three freinds Books one being Intituled to the noble Bareans of these Times the other two being a Book of Robt Barclayes work & Wm Smiths work they being all sent out of England from freinds there to freinds heare being a free Guift bestowed for Generall service heare among freinds.

the 3 of the 2 Mo 1702

And Account that freinds belonging to nansemond meeting Gives of A meeting house built by them in the southern branch of nansemond River standing on a spot of ground belonging to Levin Bufkin Plantation which meeting house is 20 foot in length & 20 foot in width & the Inside seled with Planks allso the floor laid with Plank & fitted with formes and seates the building & fitting the above sd house besides nailes Cost

3868 ℔ Tobb.

Given By the members of the above sd meeting to defray the charges of the above sd meeting house as followeth

Pr Robt Jordan	580	Given by some of
John Mardah	550	the above sd mem-
Ben. Small	520	bers of the meeting
Jno Porter	500	nailes of all sortes
Nathan Newby	500	for the building the
Jno Hollowell	350	house besides the To-
Ricd Hopkins	350	bacco given by them.
Matt Small	250	
Elizab Mace	100	
Moses Hall	350	

In all   3 :9 :50

Edmond Belson the sonn of Elizabeth Belson of Nanzemun And Mary Crew the daughter of Mary Tooke of the Isleaweight county propounded their marriage before a meeting of frends men & women at the house of William Clarkes in Pagon Creeke on the 13th day of the 9 moth Last and coming before the meeting the second time at Richard Ratlife's howse one the Eleventh day of this Instant month they did publish their marriage again and were married in the house of his mother on the 13th day of the 10th. month 1684

Edmond : Belson
Mary : Crew

Witnesses: Tho. Hodges
Mother Elizabeth Belson   John Copland
Mother Mary Tooke   Samuell Newton

James Tooke
Rodger Newham
Tho. Hollowell
Willm Newby
John Scott
Richard Ratliff
William Outeland
William Granbery
Robart Peelle
Tho. Jordan Junior
Levin Bufkin
Tho. Jordan
Robart Rowse
Will Sanders

John More
John Jordan
Allis Hollowell
Margret Jordan
Elizabeth Scott
Elizabeth Ratliff
Elizabeth Jordan
Elizabeth Hollowell
Mary Sanders
Elizabeth Ratliff yongr
Christian Outeland
Alice Hollowell
Elizabeth Copland

John Scott the sonn of William Scott of Chucatuck in the county of Nanzemun and Elizabeth Belson the daughter of Elizabeth Belson of the county aforesaid did propound their marriage before a meeting of men and women frends in Elizabeth Belsons howse aforesaid on ye eaight day of the forth Month Last, and coming before the meeting a second time at Thomas Jordans howse in Chucatuck did publish their marriage againe on the 7th seventh day of ye seventh Month last and were married in the house of his mother on the 19th day of the 8th month in the year 1682

John Scott
Elizabeth : Belson

Witnesses:
Father William Scott, Elder
Mother Elizabeth Belson
Bror Edmond Belson
Bror William Scott, Jun
Thomas Goodwin
Robt Peele
Isaac Rickes
John Chilcott
John More

Joseph Hollowell
Robt Laurence Elder
Tho: Jordan Elder
Joseph Copland
Rich: Ratliff
Will Outeland
Robt Jones
Will: Sanders
Edmund Godwin
Tho: Jordan

Rich Buxton   Eliz Copland
John Copland   Katheren Rickes
Henry Hacly   Eliz: Jordan
Eliz: Scott   Eliz: Ratliff
Margret Jordan   Mary Hodges

John Jordan the son of Thomas Jordan of Chuckatuck in ye county of Nanzemund and Margaret Burgh of ye same place did publish their marriage at a meeting of friends both men and women at Richard Ratliffs howse in ye Isle-aweight county on ye: 8th day of the tenth month last And coming before ye meeting ye second time at William Sand-erses howse in ye county aforesaid they did publish their marriage againe one the twelft day of ye Eleventh month last and were married in ye house of his father on ye Ninth day of ye twelfe month in ye year: 1688.

John Jordan
Margaret Burgh

father Tho: Jordan   Elizabeth Godwin
Mother Margaret Jordan Abagall Brassewr ante
ouncele John Brassere   Elizabeth Copland
Brother Tho Jordan Junr Elizabeth Woory
Brother Robert Jordan   Elizabeth Jordan, sister
John Copland   Margaret Davis, ante
Tho Godwin   Eliz: Ratliff, Elder
Rich: Ratliff   Sara: Sanburne
Hen: Hackley   Eliz: Newbye
Will: Newbye   Mary Bryan
ouncle James Davis   Eliz: Bradley
Robt Jones   Johe Laurence
Tho: Page   Dorithy Newbye
Leaven Bufkin   Christian Jordan sister
Joseph Jordan   Eliz Ratliff: yongr

Robart Jordan the son of Tho: Jordan of Chucatuck in ye county of Nanzemund and Christian: Oudeland ye daughter of Tho: Taberer of the Isleaweight county did publish their marriage at a meeting of men & women friends at

William Sanders his howse ye county aforesd on ye twelft day of ye Eleventh month last past And coming before ye meeting the second time in his fathers house they did publish their marriage againe on ye ninth day of this Instant month and were married in the house of his father on this Ninth day of ye twelft month in ye yeare 1687.

<table>
<tr><td></td><td>Robart: Jordan</td></tr>
<tr><td></td><td>Christian: Oudeland</td></tr>
<tr><td>father Tho: Jordan</td><td>Abagall Brassewr ante</td></tr>
<tr><td>Mother Margaret Jordan</td><td>Elizabeth Copland</td></tr>
<tr><td>ouncle John Brassewr</td><td>Elizabeth Woory</td></tr>
<tr><td>Brother Tho: Jordan, Junn</td><td>Elizabeth Jordan, sister</td></tr>
<tr><td>Tho: Godwin</td><td>Margaret Davis, ante</td></tr>
<tr><td>ouncle James Davis</td><td>Eliz: Ratliff, Elder</td></tr>
<tr><td>Brother John Jordan</td><td>Sara Sanburn</td></tr>
<tr><td>John Copland</td><td>Eliz: Newbye</td></tr>
<tr><td>Rich: Ratliff</td><td>Mary Bryan</td></tr>
<tr><td>Leaven Bufkin</td><td>Eliz: Bradley</td></tr>
<tr><td>Hen: Hackley</td><td>Jone Laurence</td></tr>
<tr><td>Will: Newbye</td><td>Christian Jordan, sister</td></tr>
<tr><td>Robt. Jones</td><td>dorrithy Newbye</td></tr>
<tr><td>Tho Page</td><td>Eliz: Ratliff, younger</td></tr>
<tr><td>Eliz: Godwin</td><td></td></tr>
</table>

Robard Jordan & his wife Christians daughters berth day & yeare

Christian Jordan the daughter of the above said was borne the 23 day of the first month in ye year 1689

And Christian Jordan ye wife of Robar Jordan died ye 26 of ye 6 mo 89

James Jordan, the sonn of Thomas Jordan of Chuckatuck in ye County of Nanzemund and Elizabeth Ratliff the daughter of Richard Ratliff of Isleaweight county did propound their marriage before a meeting of men and women friends in William Sanders his howse in Nanzemund on ye 12th day of ye Eleventh month in 1687 and coming before the meeting the second time in his fathers house they did publish their marriage againe on ye 9th day ye 12 month next after ye date above sd and were married at John Coplands howse on the 29th day of the 3 month In ye yeare 1688.

James Jordan
Elizabeth Ratliff

fathers   Tho: Jordan
    &
mothers Margaret Jordan

Rich Ratliff
Eliz: Ratliff
John Copland
Eliz. Copland
Tho Jordan Jun
John Jordan
Robart Jordan
James Davis
John Neivell
James Jordan
Joseph Copland
Tho: Godwin
Joseph Woory
Tho. Taberer
John Scott
Will: Wilkison
Edmond Belson
Thomas Page
Tho: Tooke
James Jordan, Seinr

Edmond Godwin
Tho: Davis: cuzon
John Neivell: cuzon
John Campbell
Joseph Jordan
Rich Ratliff, Junr
Daniell Accers
Elizabeth Godwin, Senr
Eliz: Neivell
Margret Davis
Eliz: Jordan
Christian Jordan
Margret Jordan
Eliz. Copland
Sara Wilkeson
Ann Cary
Eliz: Scott
Sara Sanburn
Sara Ratliff
Eliz Campbell

James Jordan & his wife Elizabeth theire childrens berths Recorded

Elizabeth ye daughter of ye afore sd James & Elizabeth his wife was borne on the ....
....

James Jordan ye sonn of ye afore sd James & Elizabeth was borne ....

And Elizabeth Jordan wife of ye Afore sd James Jordan died ye Laste of : 6 moth 1695

.   .   .   .

Leaven Bufkin & Dorrithy Newby The Daughter of William Newby of Nanzemund did propound their marriage before a meeting of friends men & women at Tho: Jordans howse in Chucatuck on ye 9th day of ye 12 moth Last and coming before the meeting the second time in Isaac Reeks howse they did publish their marriage againe on ye 12th day of this month and were married in his own house on the seventeenth day of ye second month 1688.

		Leaven Bufkin
		Dorrithy Newby
Witnesses:	John Small	Alce Hollowell
Robart Willson	Marke Alsbury	Ann Wilson
Nathan Newby	Robard Jones	Margret Jordan
Gabrell Newby	frances Mace	Eliz Scott
John Scott	John Keeton	Ann Small
Johnathan Newby	Andrew Ross	Eliz Ratliff
Edmond Belson	John Small Junir	Martha Jones
Tho: Duke	Izabell Newby	Margret Duke
Rich: Ratliff	Eliz Jordan	Mary Sanders
Christopher Gewin	Eliz: Newby	Mary Keeton
Isaac Reecks	Eliz: Copland	Ann Hacly

Leven Bufkin the sonn of the above-Sd Leven Bufkin & Dorrithy his wife was born the Eight day of the twelfe month in ye yeare—1688—

Henry Hollowell of Elizabeth River & Elizabeth Scott of Nanzemund county did propound their marriage at a meeting of men & women freinds at the howse of Thomas Tookes on the 9th day of the first month Last and at a meeting at Isaac Reecks the 13th day of this Instant thay

published there Marriage ye second time and were married
in his house on the 20th day of the 2 month: 1693

                                    Henry : Hollowell
                                    Elizabeth Scott
Witnesses: John Evans   Thomas Jordan
Nathan Newby   William Scott   Margaret Jordan
John Small   Robart Jordan   Mary Jordan
Benjamine Small   Henry Hackly   Sara Ratliff
John Mackwilliams   Thomas Duke   Elizabeth Newby
Isaac Reekesis   Robart Mountgomry Dorrithy Bufkin

.   .   .   .

John Harris & Elizabeth Church of Isleaweight county
did propound their marriage at a meeting of men & women
freinds in Isaac Reekesis howse on ye Eleventh of this second month last and coming before the meeting ye second
time in Henry Wiggs howse of ye county afore sd they did
publish there mariage againe on ye 13th day of the fourth
month and ther tooke one another in Marriage on this thirteenth day of ye forth month in ye year : 1689—

                                    John Harris
                                    Elizabeth Church
Tho: Harris   Walter Barklet   Tho Jordan
John: Morry   William Cooke   Mary Tooke
John Graue   Tho Proode   Eliz Morry
Tho: Tooke   Peeter Greefes   Sara Greefes
Tho: Page   Henry Wiggs   Jane Cooke
Edmond Prime   Isaac Rickesis

.   .   .   .

John Small the sonn of John Small of Nanzemund And
Alce Hollowell the Daughter of Alce Hollowell of Elizabeth River County did publish their marriage before a
meeting of men & women frends in Mary Sanderses howse
in Nanzemund on the tenth day of the Eleventh month last
And coming before the meeting the second time in Thomas
Jordans howse in Chucatuck they did publish their mariage againe on the fourteenth of this twelfe month and

were married in hir Mothers howse on this 25 day of ye 12th month in ye yeare 1688.

John Small
Alce Hollowell

far John Small	Tho Hodges	Tho: Jordan
mor Alce Hollowell	Edmond Belson	Sarah Howard
bror Joseph Hollowell	Tho: Page	Anie Small
bror Henry Hollowell	Henry Hackly	Martha Jones
bror Nathan Newby	Tho. Duke	Eliz: Newby
bror John Hollowell	Robt Jones	Mary Sanders
bror Benja Small	fran Mace	Margaret Jordan

· · · · · · · · · · ·

Nathan Newby the sonn of William Newby of Nanzemund County & Elizabeth Hollowell ye daughter of alce Hollowell of Elizabeth River did publish their Marriage at a meeting of men & women frends at Daniell Sanburns howse on the thirteenth day of ye Eaight month of this date and coming before the meeting the second time at William Cookes in Isleaweight county they did publish there Marriage againe on the tenth day of the ninth after and were married in hir Mothers house on this thirteenth day of the tenth month in the yeare—1687—

Nathan Newby
Elizabeth Hollowell

William Newby	Izabell Newby
Gabrell Newby	Alce Hollowell
John Hollowell	Dorrithy Newby
Thomas Page	Elizabeth Scott
John Copland	Martha Jones
ffrances Mace	Ann Hackly
John Scott	Margret Duke
Robart Jones	Elizabeth Copland
Henry Hacly	

EARLY QUAKER RECORDS IN VIRGINIA.

Robart Jordan the son of Thomas Jordan of Chucatuck in ye county of Nanzemund and Mary Belson the daughter of Edmund Belson deceased of the county aforesaid did publish there Marriage before a meeting of frends both men & women at Henry Wiggs house in ye Isleaweight county on ye twelfe day of ye fourth month last. And coming before Meeting ye second time in John Scotts house in ye county aforesd they did publish their marriage againe on ye tenth day of this Instant date and were married in John Scotts house on the tenth day of the fift month In the yeare 1690.

Robart Jordan
Mary Belson

Witnesses:

Thomas Jordan father	Eliz Scott
Margaret Jordan: Mother	Eliz Jordan sistr
Edmond Belson Bror	Tho: Tooke
Thomas: Jordan Bror	Robt: Peele yonger
Dan Bror	John Evans
James Jordan Bror	John Granberry
John: Scott Bror	William Stapells
Eliz. Scott sistr	Robart Peele Elder
Margaret Jordan, sister	And divers others

Mary Jordan the Wife of Robt Jordan Departed this Life ye 25th Day ———

John Persons ye sonn of John Persons in ye county of Isleaweight And Mary Patredg the daughter of Thomas Patredg in ye county of Sirry did publish there marriage at a meeting of frends in Richard Ratlifes howse in ye county afore sd on ye tenth day of ye tenth month last And coming before the meeting the second time in Thos Jordans

howse at Chucatuck on ye Eleventh day of ye twelft month
last they did publish there Marriage againe and were married in Thomas Tookes howse in ye Isle a weight County on
this tenth day of the first month in ye yeare 1691(2).

John Persons
Mary Patredg

John Parsons: father　　　Rubin Gladwell
Thomas Pateredg father　 William Cooke
Thomas Tooke　　　　　　 John: Cooke
Thomas Proud　　　　　　 Tho: Jordan, Senior
Walter Barklet　　　　　 Mary Tooke
John Harris　　　　　　　 Jone Cooke
Peter Greeves　　　　　　 Margret Jordan
James Tooke　　　　　　　 Eliz: Ratliff
Edmond Prime　　　　　　 Sara Ratliff
James Dickinson　　　　　 Ionas Tooke
Thomas: Wilson　　　　　 Sara Jones
Thomas Page

John Denson ye sonn of frances Denson wido woman and
Mary Brydell ye daughter of frances Bridell of Isleaweight
county did propound their marriage before a meeting of men
& women frends at ye howse of Daniell Sanburns in ye afore
sd county on ye thirteenth day of ye 8th month last past And
coming before ye meeting ye second time at William Cooks
in ye county afore sd they did publish their marriage againe
on the tenth day of this Instant month and were married
in her father's howse on the twelft day of the 9 month in ye
yeare 1692

John Denson
Mary Brydle

francis: Denson　　　John Good
frances Brydell　　　John Jordan
Mary Brydell　　　　Tho: Jordan
James Denson　　　　Kathn Reeks
Joseph Denson　　　 Margret Jordan
Thomas: Page　　　　Eliz Scott

Isaac Rickesis

Will: Rickesis

Richard Ratliff

Daniell Akehurst

Stephen: Powell

Will: Scott Elder

Tho: Exam Justis

Sara Sanburn

Mary Brydell

Eliz: Ratliff

Eliz Scott, yonr

Alce Page

Sara Barnes

Joseph Merrideth the sonn of Samson Merrideth of Nansemund county did publish his intentions of marriage wth Sarah Denson ye daughter of ffrancis Denson of Isleaweight county in our public Meeting ye 14th day of ye 3rd month last past: And likewise ye 2d time at freinds Monthly meeting at Henry Wiggs hows in ye Isleaweight county and were married on this 11th day of ye 4th month : 1696

Joseph Merrideth

Sarah Denson

Mor ffrancis: Denson

James: Denson

John: Denson

Tho: Jordan

John: Harris

Tho: Proud

Henry Wiggs

Edmond Prime

William Cooke

James Jordan

John Jordan

Joseph Jordan

Rich: Ratliff

Benjamine Small & Elizabeth Hallowell of Nanzemund county propounded their marriage before a meeting of friends both men & women in ye publick Meeting howse at Chuckatuck on ye ninth day of the twelfth month last and coming before the Meeting the second time in ye publick meeting howse at chuckatuck they did publish their marriage againe on the ninth day of this Instant and were married in ye sd meeting howse on this twelft day of ye first month—1699

Benjamine Small

Elizabeth Hollowell

Edmond Belson

Robart Jordan

Joshua Jordan

James Munkly

John Small   Alice Small
Mathew Small   Margret Jordan
John Jordan   Elizabeth Porter
James Jordan   Kathern Bullock
Benjamine Jordan   Jean Belson
Samuell Jordan   Elizabeth Hollowell
William Scott   Mary Ratliff

Joseph Kenerly of Dorchester county in the province of
Maryland And Sara Ratliff the daughter of Richard Ratliff of Isleaweight county in Virginia did publish their Intentions of Marriage at a quarterly meeting of men & women freinds held at william Scotts howse in ye Isleaweight
county afore sd on the Eleventh day of ye sixth month last
and on the twenty first following they did publish there intentions of Marriag againe ye 2d time before friends in there
publick Meeting howse at Chucatuck And on ye Eleventh
day of this Instant date they did publish theire Marriage ye
3d time before all freinds and people at the yearly Meeting
in Freinds Meeting howse in ye Isleaweight county and were
married before a congregation of friends and people in
Chucatuck Public Meeting howse on this 20th of ye 7 month
1696.

Joseph Kenerly
Sarah Ratliff

Witnesses:
far Richard Ratliff   Robart Jordan
John Copland   Joseph Jordan
Richard Ratliff   Eve Bellonge
Thomas Page   William Powell
Isaac Reekes   Cornelius Ratliff
William Yearly   Eliz: Ratliff
Henry Wilkison   Mary Ratliff
Mark Alsbury   Margaret Jordan
Thomas Jordan   Mary Alsbury
John Jordan   Mary Copland
James Jordan   ffrances Wilkison

Edward Belson of Nanzemund in Virginia and Joan Ridick the daughter of Robart Ridick of the same county did make publication of their Intentions of marriage before a meeting of friends men & women at ye howse of Allice Hollowell upon ye ninth day of the third month last past and coming before the Meeting the second time at the howse of John Scott on the Eleventh day of this Instant they did publish theire Marriage againe and were there married on this 11th day of ye 5 moth 1689

Edmond Belson
Jean Ridick

Witnesses:

John Scott	Thomas Page
Elizabeth Scott	Thomas Coward
Elizabeth Ridick	John Small
Sara Coward	Robart Montgumry
Mary Ridick	Robart Jones
Thomas Bullard	Henry Hackly
John Evans	Richart Ratliff
Thomas Duke	William Scott
Nathan Newly	John Jordan
ffrances Mace	Margaret Jordan
Thomas Jordan	James Jordan
Eve belonge	Elizabeth Newby
Robart Peelle	

Thomas Newman & Mary Ratliff of Isleaweight county did propound their marriage before a meeting in ye publick meeting howse at Chucatuck on ye 9th day of ye 12th month last and coming before ye meeting the 2nd time in ye sd meeting howse they did publish their Marriage againe and were there married on this 13th day of ye 2d month: 1699.

Thomas Newman
Mary Newman

Witnesses:

Richard Ratliff	John Jordan
Thomas Page	Sara Sanburn

John Porter	Elizabeth Sanburn
James Munkley	Isabell Newman
Benjamine Small	Margaret Jordan: Elder
James Jordan	Margaret Jordan: youngr
John Ratliff	Thomas Jordan

Mathew Jordan the sonn of Thomas Jordan of Chucatuck & Dorrity Bufkin widdo woman both of Nanzemund county did propound theire Marriage before a meeting of men & women friends in the publick Meeting howse at chucatuck on the 10th of ye sixt month last And coming before the Meeting the second time in the generall meeting howse thay did publish there marriage againe and were married this 6th day of ye 7th month 1699

Mathew Jordan
Dorrithy Jordan

Witnesses:

father Thomas Jordan	Sisters Margaret Jordan
John Jordan	Daniell Sanburn
James Jordan	Richard Ratliff
Bro. Robard Jordan	John Campbell
thers Richard Jordan	Abraham Rickes
Benjamine Jordan	William Page
Samuell Jordan	Mary Copland
Joshua Jordan	Sara Sanburn
Mother Margaret Jordan	Eliz: Sanburn
Elizabeth Jordan	

Jacob Rickesis the son of Isaac Rickesis And mary Exum the Daughter of Jeremiah Exum both of the county of the Isle weight propounded their marriage before A meeting of men & women freinds at our Publick meeting house in Chuckatuck on the ninth day of the ninth mo 1699 last past and coming before the meeting the second time at our pub-

lick meeting house in Chucatuck on the 14 day of the 10 mo
1699 were married

Jacob Rickesis
Mary M Exum

Isaac Rickesis   Jno Rickesis
James Denson   Abraham Rickesis
John Denson   Richd Exum
Daniel Sanbourn   ffrancis Denson
Thomas Page   Mary Lawrence
Richd Rattcliff   Joane Lawrence
Jno Rattcliff   Elizabeth Lawrence
ffrances Bridle   Sarah Sanbourn
Nathan Newby   Sarah Horning
Henry Wiggs   Elizabeth Rattcliff

Thomas Gay son of Isaac Lawrence & Rebecca Page the
Daughter of Thomas Page both of the county of the Ile of
weight did propound their marriage before a meeting of
men & women freinds at our publick meeting house in Chuckatuck the 14 day of the 10 mo last past and coming
before the meeting the second time they Published their
marriage againe and at our above sd Publick meeting house
were married this 11th day of the 11th mo In the year 1699

Thomas Gay
Rebecca Page

Thomas Page Senor   Daniel Sanbourn
Isaac Rickesis Senor   Alce Page
Nathan Nuby   Joane Lawrence
Robt Lawrence Junor   Jane Sikes
Mark Alsbury   Elizabeth Powell
Henry Wilkinson   Sarah Sanbourn
Wm Powell

Wm Powel the son of Elizabeth Powel widdow and mary
Page the daughter to Thomas Page both within the Pre-
cincts of the Ile of weight did propound their marrage before a meeting of men and women freinds At our Publick

meeting howse in Chuckatuck on the 14 day of the first mo
1700 last past And coming before the meeting the second
time at our above sd Publick meeting house in Chuckatuck
they did publish their marriage againe Itt being on the 11th
day of the 2 mo 1700 and were married in her fathers
Thomas Pages house this 14 day of the 2 mo In yeare 1700

Wm Powell

the mark of

Mary X Page

Thomas Page	Tho: Gay
Isaac Rickesis	Abra Rickesis
John Rickesis	Marke Alsebury
Jacob Rickesis	Alice Page
Jno Simmons	Elizabeth Powel widdow
James Munckly	Mary Lawrence widdow
Nathan Newby	Joane Lawrence
ffrancis Bridle	Kathren Rickesis
Richd Turner	Rebecca Gay

Richd Rattclif the sonn of Richd Rattclif senior of the
Trevascoenecks and Eizabeth Hollowell daughter of Henry
Hollowell deceased of the Ile of weight county did propound
their marriage before a meeting of men & women freinds at
our Publick meeting House in Chucatuck Itt being one the
tenth day of the sixth mo last Past and coming before the
meeting the second time at our above sd meeting house on
the 11 day of the 7 mo they did publish their marriage againe
And were married in his father Richd Ratclifs owne house
on this 18 day of the 7th mo In the yeare : 1700

Richd Rattcliff

Elizabeth Hollowell

Richd Rattcliff father	John Ratcliff
Wm Scott	Isaac Rickesis
Jno Green	Daniel Sanbourn
Jno Jordan	mother Elizabeth Rattclif
James Jordan	Margaret Jordan Senior
Tho Page	Margaret Jordan Junior

Robt Jordan   Rachel White
Joshua Jordan   Rebecca Rattclif sister

On the 14 day of the 7 mo in the year 1701 James Jordwin
And Jane Roseter of Elizabeth River Took Each other In
Marriage
. . . .
Thomas Page the son of Thomas Page of the western
Branch of the Ile of weight County and Isabell Lawrence
Daughter to Henry Lawrence of the western branch of the
County of Nansemund did propound their marriage at a
meeting of men & women freindes at our Publick meeting
House in Chuckatuck on the 12 day of the 12 mo 1701 and
coming before the meeting the second time at our above sd
meeting house in Chuckatuck at a meeting of men & women
friendes they did publish their marriage againe on the 12
of the first mo 1702 and were married in the house of Frances
Denson widdow the 15 day of this Instant mo being the
first mo of the year 1702—

the mark of
Thomas T P Page
the mark of
Isabell I P Lawrence

Witnesses:
father Thomas Page   Wm Scot
Isaac Rickesis Senior   Alice Page, mother
John Rickesis   Elizabeth Lawrence
Broes Michall Lawrence   Joane Lawrence
Tho Lawrence   Mary Lawrence
Wm Scote, Senior   Rebecca Gay
Wm Scot   Alice Powell

. . . .
Mathew Jordan of the County of Nanzemond and Susan-
na Bresy widdow of the County of the Ile of weight did propound their marriage before a meeting of men and women
friendes in the Publick meeting house at Chuckatuck on the

12 day of the first mo in the year 1702 and coming before the meeting the second time and at our Above sd Public meeting house Itt being on the 14 day of the 3 mo in the above sd year and were married Before a meeting of friendes In the Leavyneeck meeting house on the seaventeenth day of the 3 mo in the year 1702

Mathew Jordan
Susanna Bresy

Witnesses:

John Harris
Henry Wigges
Hugh Bresy
John Moory
John Brett
Isaac Rickesis, Senior
Thomas Newman
John Harrison

Levin Buffkin.
Wm Harrison
Sarah Bresy
Elizabeth Gayner
Elizabeth Harris
Kathren Wiggs
Alse Blake

EARLY QUAKER RECORDS IN VIRGINIA.

Abraham Rickesis the sonn of Isaac Rickesis of the western Branch of Nanzemond River & Mary Bellson the Daughter of Edmond Bellson of Nanzemond County did Propound their marriage Before a meeting of men and women friends at our Publick meeting House in Chuckatuck on the eight day of the 2 mo last past and coming before the meeting above sd the second time upon the 13 day of this Instant they did againe publish their marriage and were married at our Publick meeting house on the western Branch of nanzemond on the 16 day of the 3 : mo In the year 1703.

Abraham Rickesis.
Mary Bellson.

Witnesses:

father Isaac Rickesis	Kathren Rickesis, mother
Bro John Rickesis	Elizabeth small, Ante
Bro Robert Rickesis	Mary Jordan Ante
Bro Jacob Rickesis	Elizabeth scot senior
Uncell Wm Scot, senior	ffrancis Denson
uncell Benmin Small	Elizabeth scot, Junior
Tho Page	Joan Lawrence
Jno Denson	Mary Lawrence
Jno Simons	Rebecca Rattliff
ffrancis Hutchins	

George Murrell sonn of George Murrell of the county of surry & mary waters the daughter of walter waters of the County of the Isle of weight did propound their Marriage before A meeting of men & women friends at our Publick meeting house in Chuckatuck on the 9 day of the first mo in the year 1703 last Past and coming before the meeting the second time at our above sd Public meeting house on the 13 day of this Instant 2 mo they did publish their marriage againe and were married at our Public meeting House In the western branch of nansemond River on this 16 day of this Instant 2 mo as in the year 1704

George Murrell
Mary Waters

Witnesses:
father Walter Waters
father George Murrell   Elizabeth murrell, mother
Tho Page   Sarah Horning
Mark Alsbury   Anne Exum
Isaac Rickesis   Elizabeth Exum
Abraham Rickesis   Elizabeth Hampton
Wm Pope   Mary Rickesis
Richd Turner   Mary Rickesis
Robt Rickeis   Willmeth Gabis

ffrom our mans meeting held at Chuckatuck on the 14 day 7 mo 1704 the Defference depending between Jeremiah Exum & Isaac Rickes senior is finally ended upon this Proviser Isaac Rickes Junor & Robt Rickes his Bror hath each of them alike past their obligation for two Thousand pounds of Tobbacs to the widdow namely Mary Rickes the widdow of Jacob Rickes deseased wch is done in lieu of his Childrens part or potion of land or anything els wch may be claimed after the desease of the sd Isaac Rickes senior And wee are wittenes of the same whoses names are heare Inserted

nathan newby   Daniel Sanbourn
Jno Porter   Jno small
Beniamin small   Jno Murdah

from our mens meeting at our meeting House at Chuckatuck in ye County of nancemond virginia held the 8 day of the first mo 170¾

To the monthly meeting of friends belonging to Pequinans in north Carolina Dear friends after our loves to you all Remembd desireing your prosperitie the everlasting & unchangabel truth of God desireing that therein both you & wee may bee kept to ye end of our daies & friends as wee

hear dwell & abide wee shall bee willing to bee helpful one
to another & shall bee ready to serve one another in the
truth of our Lord God Dear friends this is to lett you know
that wee Recd youres & Robt willsons will Itt hath been
Read in our mens meeting in weightyly Considered wee
hoape in the fear of God & weyed in the ballance of Equitie
& it is the Judgment of our meeting that Isaac willson ought
to pay the 18 pounds given by Robt willson ye testator to
sarah Bellman or to her heires lawfully begotten Provided
that John Bellman husband to sarah bellman doe give in bond
& securitie to Isaac willson that if Jno Bellmans daughter or
daughters doe inivy part of that land with Isaac's daughter or
daughters for want of and heir male of Isaac Willson to in-
herit ye land given by the Testator that ye mony bee paid
back by bellman or his heires to Isaac Willson or to his heires

Signed by order of our meeting

Pr Isaac Rickesis

Heare follows and Accompt of friends sufferings in Virginia
nansemund 1701 Margaret Jordan the Elder widdow on the
25 day of the first mo had a hundred & twenty pounds of
Tobb Taken by distress from her upon Accompt of the
Priests dews pr George noseworthy high shriff
Recd of Robt Jordan all his Levis for this present year except ten pounds of Tobb for wch I have made distress for
upon his Refusall of payment of the same I say Recd pr Frau
Millorer nansemond County 25 of the 1ober 1700

Robt Jordan is dr In 1700—to 3 Levis at a 100 pr pole
is in all ——— 300 the Priests dues of this accompt taken by
distress the Remaining pt paid per Jno Iles sub shriff the
finfth day of Aprill in the year 1701 distress was made per
Jno Iles nansemond County

April the 10 : 1702
Then seased one hogd of Tobb weghing Gros 830 : tare 75 of
mis Margaret Jordan senor for priests dewes and Church
Rates in full I say seased by mee   John King

ffebr the 18 1701
then seased Beniamin small Two hundred & twenty Two

Poundes of Tobb itt being for Priests dewes & Church rates
& to Two hundred & twenty Two Poundes of Tobb for your
fine by Capt Hanell I say Recd pr mee wch In all makes up
the sume of 444 ℔ Jno King sub shriff

By six weekes Imprisonmt for being Taken Att A meeting in my owne house & Released by the Kings Proclama-
tion 2 by taken at a meeting at Robt Lawrence & bound over
to the Court of nansemond who for Refusing to swear according to their wills & agt the Comand of Christ was sent
up to Jamestowne A Prisoner upwards of Ten monthes
Presently After John Blake Took Away my 3 servants And
left my wife in a Distressed Condition with A young Child
sucking at her Brests that to help her selfe the Child did
burst Itselfe with Crying wch servants were kept about nine
weekes and then Returned Againe by the Governors order
Taken by distress by Jno Blake hie shrieff of nansemond
County two feather beds and three feather Boulsters & fur-
niture to them with other Goods wch did Amount to (3907
Pounds of Tobacco & also a servant man that had three
yeares to serve taken by John Blake Taken by destress by
Thomas Godwin shrieff ten head of Cattells And delivered
to Wm stinton of James Town the sufferings of the Goodes
did amount to

3907 by Aprisment
the servants to 1600   Tho Jordan

In all   5507
the Chattells I have no Accompt of
    Chuckatuck dated the first of ye 7 mo 1664
    Aprill the 2 1703 then seased from James Jordan 35 ∴
pounds Tobb for the Priests dewes & Church Rates pr mee
                                        John Watts
                                            sub shrif
    of Richard Rattcliff sesed by vertue of & execution 179 :
pounds of Tobb for the use of Thomas Pitt bearing date
January ye 25 1703   Geo Green sub shrif

I doe hereby accquit & discharge Richd Rattcliff from all Judgmts executions or Debts whatsoever Pr Henry Pitt

ffebr 24 : 170 2-3

Sesed by Tho Pitt high shrif of the Ile white County 1703 the sume of 160 ℔ of Tobb for the Priest Andrew monroe & other Church rates to wit Clerk saxton

from Pr Richd Rattcliff senior

ffebr the 24 day 1704

Then seased & Carried Away one 179 pounds of Tobb from Richd Rattcliff itt being for power parrish levies I say Recd   pr Jno watts

Richd Jordan the sonn of Thomas Jordan of Chuckatuck deceased & Rebecca Rattcliff the Daughter of Richd Rattcliff of the Trevascoe necks did Publish their marriage Before a meeting of men & women friends in our Public meeting house in Chuckatuck on the eleaventh day of the 5 mo in the year 1706 And coming before the meeting the second time at our mo meeting held at our Publick meeting House upon the eight day of the 6 mo following they did publish their marriage the second time and were married in the house of Richd Rattcliff Rebecca Rattcliff father on the 22 day of the sixth mo in the year 1706

Richd Jordan
Rebecca Jordan

Richd Rattcliff father	
Beniamin Jordan Bro	Benia Small
Jno Jordan Bro	Robt Rickes
Robt Jordan Bro	Mattw Small
Joshua Jordan Bro	Elizabeth Rattcliff mother
James JordanBro	Margaret Jordan mother
Richd Rattcliff Bro	Mary Jordan
Jno Ratcliff Bro	Margret Jordan
Thomas Page	Elizabeth Small
Nathan Newbye	Elizabeth Newby
Jno Small	Alse Small
Wm Scot	Sarah Sanbourn

Wm Pope of the County of nanzemond and Mary Haile of the County aforesd did Publish their marriage In our Publick meeting house Before a meeting of men & woman friends upon the 11 day of the first mo 1707 and Coming Before the meeting the second time att our aforesd Publick meeting house in Chuckatuck upon the eight Day of the 2 mo 1708 they did publish their marriage the second time and were married in the Public meeting house on the western Branch on the eleaventh day of the 2 mo 1708

Wm Pope
Mary Pope

Bro Henry Pope	Thomas Page
Jno Porter	Wm Powell
Jno Asken	Rebecca Alsbury
Robt Rickes	Sarah Pope
Isaac Rickes	Elizabeth Powell
Phillip Alsbury	Kathren Rickes

Wm Scott the sonn of John Scott of the County of nansemond Deceased And Christian Jordan the Daughter of Robt Jordan of the County Aforesd did Publish their marriage Before a meeting of men and woman friends at our Publick meeting House in Chuckatuck on the 10 day of the 5 mo last Past and Coming Before the meeting the second time at our aforesd Publick meeting House in Chuckatuck on the the 14 day of the 6 mo last past they did publish their marriage the second time and were married in the house of her Grandmother Margaret Jordan widdow of Chuckatuck on this 28 day of the 6 mo In the year 1707

William Scott
Christian Scot

Witnesses:

Mother Eliz Small	Tho Newman
Grandmother Margaret Jor- dan	Is Rickes
Benia Jordan	Richd Rattliff
	John Rattliff

Jno Jordan   Joshua Jordan
Richd Jordan   James Jordan
Eliz Jordan   Sarah Sanburn

James Denson the sonn of ffrances Denson of the Ilse wight County widdow woman and Sarah Dryton (?) of the County Aforesd did Publish their marriage Before a meeting of men & woman friends at our Publick meeting House in Chuckatuck on the 13 day of the 9 mo 1707 and coming Before the meeting A second and A third time at our aforesd Publick meeting House did publish againe and were married In the Publick meeting House in the western Branch on this 15 day of the 11 mo 1707

James Denson
Sarah Denson

Witnesses:

Joseph Meredith   ffrances Bridle
Jno Denson   Thomas Page
Jere Exum   Robt Horning
Isaac Rickes   Elizabeth Lawrence
Robt Lawrence   Elizabeth Brian
Lewis Brian   Elizabeth Powell
Wm Brian   Anne Exum

EARLY QUAKER RECORDS IN VIRGINIA.

And Account of our meeting House being Built By friends In the western Branch of nanzemond River in the year 1702 and is now sett upon a spott of Ground wch friendes did Purchase of francis Hutchins the elder being twenty five foott in length & twenty foott in width fitted every way with formes & Benches sutable for such A House the workmen's demand due to them for their worke building the s^d House is three Thousand Pounds of Tobb.

Given by us the Members of the s^d meeting in the Above s^d year to witt As follows:

	℔ Tobb
Isaac Rickes Senior	400
Wm Scott Senior	400
James Denson	400
Jno Denson	300
Abrah^m Rickes	100
Jno Rickes	100
Robt Rickes	100
Jno Sikes	150
Thos Hampton	200
ffrances Denson	500
	2650

wch in all makes 2650

ffrancis Bridle did Give Nayles toward the building this house

Sence the House is finished there hath been another Collection made so as to Compleat the above ^{sd} sume of Tobb wch is 3200 Pounds wth wch is the workmen due wch by name is Abraham Rickes & Rob Rickes

Francis Braise of the Isle white County: and Son of Huge

Braise of yᵉ saime County Planter: and Elizabeth wiggs
Daughter of Henry wiggs: of yᵉ afore sd County deceased
having declared their marriage before several publick meetings of yᵉ people called Quakers in Virgᵃ the sd francis
Braise and Elizabeth wiggs afore sd were married in ye
publick meeting house at Leave Neck on the fiveteen day of
yᵉ seventh month in yᵉ yeare according to yᵉ Inglish aCount
one thousand seven hundred and thirteen

Witnesses:	ffrancis Braisse
John Scott	the E mark
Blackebe Terill	of Eliz wiggs
Willᵐ Harrison	
Joan Scott	
Willᵐ Harrison	
George wiggs	
Sarah wiggs	
Katherine Scott	

Cornelious Ratcliff of the Ile of white County & Eliz. Jordan widow of the affore sᵈ County having declared their intentions of marriage Before Several Publick meetings of
the people Called Quakers in virginia were married in a
Publick meeting att Chucatick the Twenty Third Day of the
ninth month in the year 1721

Cornelious Ratcliff
Elizabeth Ratcliff

Witnesses:	
Robert Jordan	Robert Jordan Junʳ
James Jordan	Wᵐ Scott
Benjᵃ Small	Rachel White
Wᵐ Oudlant	Sarah Wilkinson

William Denson son of John Denson of the Ile of white
County and Anney Small Daughter of Benj Small of nanse-
mond County having declared their Intentions of Taking
Each other In marriage Before several publick meetings of

the people called Quakers in virginia were married at a publick meeting of the affore s^d People and Others mett to-
gether att the house of Benj Small on This 20th Day of ye
12 mo. 172¾:

                              Wm Denson
                              Anney Denson

Witnesses:
James Copland Junr   Abra: Rix
John Denson   Francis Denson
Mary Wright   James Denson
Mourning Scott   Joseph Jordan
Ailis Small   Robt Jordan Junr
Elis Scott   Wm Scott
Mary Scott y^st   Benj Small
Tho. Gale   Benj Small Ju^r
Jn° Tillaway   John Small
Samuel Newby   Thos Small
Nathan Newby

Thomas White of The Ileofwhite county son of Jn°
White and Rachel Jordan Daughter of Joha* Jordan of
The sd County having declared their intentions of taking
Each other In marriage Before several Publick meetings
of the People called Quakers in virginia were married in a
Publick meeting of friendes in The sd County on this thir-
teenth Day of the Seventh month in the year one Thousand
Seven hundred and nineteen

                              Thomas White
                              Rachel White

Witnesses:
James Jordan   Sarah Sanburn
Mathew Jordan   Eliz Jordan
Robt Jordan Junr   Eliz Scott
Joseph Jordan   Sarah White

---

* From other sources it appears that this name should be Joshua.
The letter s was probably omitted by the recorder.

Robert Jordan   Mary Jordan
Thomas Pleasants   John Jordan
Jacob Barns   John Jordan
Cornelious Ratcliff   Saml Cornwell
Wm Scott

John Page of the Ilofwhite county and ffelicia Hall
Daughter of moses Hall Late of nansem^d County Deseaced
did publish their intentions of marriage att two several
monthly meetings of the People called Quakers in virg^a
and were married att the close of a Publick meeting for Di-
vine worship held att our meeting house w^t Branch of Nan-
sem^d (no date given)

                                 John Page
                                 ffilicia Page
Moses Hall   Thos Vann
Wm Scott   Margrett Knox
John Denson   Elis Ailsberry
Abraham Rix   Mary Scott
Wm Denson   Rebecca Ailsberry
Phil Ailsbury   Mourning Scott
Jame Lawrence   Sarah Denson
John Powel   Eliz. Rix
John Williams   Mary Powel
John Simons   Joseph Jordan, minister

Joseph Jordan son of Joseph Jordan of North Carolina
& Mary Rix daughter of Abraham Rix of Ileofwhite County
having declared their Intentions of Taking Each other In
marriage Before several Publick meetings of The People
called Quakers in Virginia, on the 10th Day of the 2nd mo.
1723 were married at a publick meeting in the sd county

                                 Joseph Jordan
                                 Mary Jordan
Witnesses:
Phlichristi Jordan   Joseph Jordan
Mary Rix   Nathan Newby

Mirrain Jordan

Mary Jordan

John Page

Wm Denson

Wm Scott

Abraham Rix

Robt Jordan Junr

Abra Tarrinson

Robt Rix

John Denson

Wm Scott

Wm Williams

Elis Jordan

Elis Rix

Sarah Denson

Elis Scott

William Wilkinson son of Henry Wilkinson of Nansem^d County Deceased and Rebeca Powel Daughter of Wm Powel of Ileofw^t County having declared their Intentions of taking Each other in marriage Before several Publick meetings of the People called Quakers In virginia were married on the 21 Day of the 9 mo in the year according to the English acct 1723 att west Branch

William Wilkinson

Rebecca Wilkinson

Witnesses:

John Denson

John Page

Jno Page

Wm Denson

Robert Scott

Eliz Scott

Mary Gay

Mary Powel

Robt Jordan Junr

John Powel

John Wilkinson

Jacob Wilkinson

Wm Scott

Wm Scott

Abraham Rix

Jane Baker

Rebeca Elsbury

Joseph Small son of John Small and Ann Owen Daughter of Gilbert Owen Both of Nansemond County declared their Intentions of Taking Each other in marriage Before several monthly meetings of the People calld Quakers in virginia and were married at a publick meeting in sd county on the 18 Day of October 1722

Joseph Small

Ann Small

Witnesses:

Tho. Small

Leav Buffkin

Nath Newby

John Murdaugh

Joseph Jordan

Ephraim Blanchard

Wm Scott

Benj Small

Matt Small

Benj Small Jn^r

Thomas Hollowell

Martha Sanders

Rachel Pearson

Mary Gay

Mary Wright

John Small

Ailis Small

William Bogue of North Carolina and Sarah Duke Daughter of Thomas Duke Late of Nansemond County Deceased Published their Intentions of taking Each other in marriage Before several meetings of the people called Quakers, and were married in a publick meeting of the afforesd people near John murdaughs in the County afforesd, on the fifteenth Day of the 12 mo 1727-8

Wm Bogue

Sarah Bogue

Mirrain Murdaugh

Martha Sanders

Elis Small

Ann Pleasants

Judith Murdaugh

Rebecca Duke

Robt Jordan Junr

Benj Small

John Jordan

John Sanders

John Wright

Leavin Buffkin

John Murdaugh

Ben Chapman on 12 of the 3 mo. 1703, condemned his having taken Mary Copland to wife [date not mentioned] contrary to the good order of Friends.

Tho. Page on 9 day of the 10 mo 1705, expressed regret for "being a subscriber to Thomas sikes his Certificate of marriage" [date of said marriage and name of the bride not mentioned].

[From this point on, the Records are copied from the other end of the same original book.—See p. 220 of this volume of the PUBLICATIONS.]

Heare is registered the Nativittys of ffreinds Children, according as their parents did give in in wrighting—

Thomas Hollowell of Elisabeth river and Alice* his wife their Childrens Nativittys recorded as followeth:

Sarah Hollowell, daughter of the aforesd Thomas & Alice* borne the first of 11 month 1647.

Thomas Hollowell, sonn of the aforesd Thomas & Alice* was borne the 22th of the first month 1649.

Henry Hollowell, sonn of the aforesd Thomas & Alice* was borne the 18th of the 8th month 1652.

John Hollowell, sonn of the aforesd Thomas & Alice* was borne the 22th of 4th month 1655, and departed this life, the 10th of the 3rd month 1671.

Joseph Hollowell, sonn of the aforesd Thomas & Alice* was borne the 15th of the 6th month 1657.

Beniamine Hollowell, sonn of the aforesd Thomas & Alice* was borne the 28th of 12 month 1659.

Elizabeth Hollowell daughter of the aforesd Tho: & Alice* was borne the 9th of the 7th month 1662.

Alise Hollowell, daughter of the aforesd Thomas & Alice* was borne the 16th of the 12 month 1664.

Edmond Hollowell sonn of the aforesd Tho: & Alice* was born the 15th of the 9th month 1667.

---

*Elizabeth has been erased and Alice substituted.

John Hollowell, sonn of the aforesd Tho: & Alice* was borne the 5th of the 9th month 1672.

William Yarrett† & Margrett his wife, their childrens Nativitties recorded as followeth,—

Katheren Yarrett, daughter of the aforesd Will. & Margrett was borne the first of the 3 month 1651.

William Yarrett, sonn of the aforesd Will, & Margrett, was borne the 5th of 9th month 1656.

Elizabeth Yarrett, daughter of the aforesd Will, & Margrett, was borne the 15th of the 3d month 1658.

Margrett Yarrett, daughter of the aforesd Will, & Margrett, was borne the first day of the last month 1664.

Margrett‡ Tabberer, wife to Thomas Tabbarer of the Ile of wight County; the nativitty of her Children recorded as followeth.,

Elizabeth Wood, daughter of the aforesd Margrett‡ Tabbarer, which shee bare to her first husband John Wood, was borne the 27th of the 7 month 1656.

Christian¶ Tabbarer, daughter of the aforsd Margrett‡ which shee bare to Thomas Tabbarer her second husband was borne in the 9th month 1661.

---

*Elizabeth has been erased and Alice substituted.

† In *Southern Quakers and Slavery* this name is given as William Parratt, but in this Register it appears frequently and always as either Yarrett or Yarratt.

‡ Elizabeth erased and Margrett written above.

¶ Margrett erased and Christian written above.

Elizabeth* Tabberer, daughter of the aforesd Margrett†
which shee bare to Thomas Tabbarer was borne the last of
the 10th month 1663.

William Denson & ffransis his wife, their Childrens Nativities recorded as followeth.,—

ffransis Denson daughter of the aforsd William & ffrancis was borne the first of the last month 1651.

William Denson sonn of the aforesd Will. & ffrancis was
borne the 25th of the 11th month, 1653.

James Denson, sonn of the aforesd Will & ffrancis was
borne the 11th of the eight month 1657.

Katheren Denson daughter of the aforesd Will & ffrancis
was borne the fowerth of the eight month 1659.

Sarah Denson, daughter of the aforesd Will. & ffrancis
was borne fowreteenth of the 11th month 1663.

John Denson sonn of the aforesd Will & ffrancis was
borne the five & twentie day of 3d month 1666.

Joseph Denson sonn of the aforesd Will & ffransis was
borne the eighteenth of 8th month 1669.

Henry Wiggs, & Katheren Yarrett, tooke each other in
mariage in the Gennerall meeting house at Chuckatuc upon
the 3rd day of the 12 month 1674 amongst a gennerall
meeting of ffreinds.

Cornelius Outland tooke Hannah Copeland to wife at a

---

*Christian erased and Elizabeth written above.
† Elizabeth erased and Margrett written above.

Gennerall meeting, & in the Gennerall meeting house at Chuckatuck [upon the 5 day of the 3 Mo 1675.*]

Wm Pope & Marie his wife their childrens Nattivitties recorded as followeth.—

Wm Pope, sonn of the aforesd W^m & Mary was borne the 15th of the 8th month 1662.

Henry Pope, sonn of th eaforesd W^m & Mary was borne the last of the 11th mo: 1663.

Alse Pope daughter of the aforesd W^m & Mary was borne of the 8 mo: 1667.

John Pope sonn of the aforesaid W^m & Mary was borne the 6th of the 8 mo 1670.

Jn° Kensy of Carolina & Katharine his wife their son^s nativitie Recorded

Jn° Kensy the son of the above sd Jn° Kensy & Katharin his wife was born on the sixth day of the tenth mo in the year 1692.

---

* Half a page following the word Chuckatuc has been cut out, the words given above in brackets have been added by a subsequent recorder.

EARLY QUAKER RECORDS IN VIRGINIA.

Richard Ratcliff of Chuckatuc his Childrens Nativities recorded

Elizabeth Ratcliff daughter of the aforesd Richard was borne the 21st of 7th mo: 1668.

Sarah Ratcliff daughter of the aforesd Richard was borne the 19th of the 9th mon; 1670.

Richard Ratcliff sonn of the aforesd Richard was borne the 13th of the 7th mon 1672.

Cornelius Ratcliff sonn of the aforesd Richard was borne the 15th of the first mon 1674-5.

Mary Rattcliff daughter of the sd Rich & Elizabeth was borne the 5 day of the 2 mo 1679.

John Ratliff ye sonn of Richard Ratliff was born ye 20th of ye 2d month in ye year: 1681.

Rebeca: Ratlif daughter of ye aforesd Richar Ratliff was borne the third day of the of ye fift month in the year 1684.

Thomas Duke his Children nativities Recorded

Thomas Duke: sonn to the aforesd Thomas Duke borne the 7th day of the 6th month 1671.

Mary Duke: daughter to the aforesd Thomas Duke borne: the 10th day of the 10th month 1674:

Edmond Belson of Nansemund & Elizabeth his wife theire Childrens Nativities Recorded as followeth........

1 Edmond Bellson sonn of ye afore sd Edmond: & Elizabeth was borne Eleventh day of ye Ninth month in ye yeare: 1664.

2 Elizabeth Bellson daughter of ye afore sd Edmond & Elizabeth was borne the Last day of ye sixt moth in ye yeare: 1666

3 Mary Bellson was borne ye: 24th day of ye: 3d moth in
ye yeare: 1673

[Isaac Rickesis And Kathren his wife their Children nativities as ffollows
Isaac Rickesis son of the afors Is & Kathren was born the
17 day of the sixth month in the year 1669.
Wm Rickesis son of the sd Is & Kathren was born the 5
day of the 8 Mo 1670.
Jn° Rickesis son of the sd Is & Kathren was born the 30
of the 10 Mo 1672
Abraham Rickesis son of the sd Is & Kathren was born
the 3 day of 10 Mo 1674
Jacob Rickesis son of the sd Is & Kathren was born the
17 day of the first 1677.
Robt Rickesis son of the sd Is & Kathren was born the 14
day of 10 Mo 1679]†
ffreinds Booke of Records per Mee Isaac Rickesis in the
year 1700.

Thomas Jordan & Margrett his wife their Childrens Nativitties Recorded as followeth in Chucatuc
1 Thomas Jordan sonn of ye afore sd Thomas & margrett
was borne ye: 6th day of ye first month in ye yeare: 1660
2 John Jordan sonn of ye aforesd Thomas & Margrett
was borne ye 17 day of the sixt month in ye yeare 1663.
3 James Jordan sonn of ye afore sd Thomas & margrett
was borne ye 23d day of the Eleventh month in ye yeare
1665
4 Robart Jordan sonn of ye aforesd Thomas & margrett
was borne ye 11 day of the seventh month in ye yeare: 1668
5 Richard Jordan sonn of ye afore sd Thomas & margrett was borne ye 6:day of the sixt month in ye yeare 1670.

† The above entries in brackets have been erased in the original
but are still legible.
The births of these children are recorded again further on in a
different handwriting.

6 Joseph Jordan sonn of ye afore sd Thomas & margrett was borne ye 8 day of the seventh month in ye yeare. 1762

7 Beniamine Jordan sonn of ye afore sd Thomas: & margrett was borne ye: 18 day of the seventh month in ye yeare —1674.

8 Maththew. Jordan sonn of ye afore sd Thomas: & Margrett was borne ye 1 day of the Eleventh month in ye yeare: 1676.

9 Samuell Jordan sonn of ye afore sd Thomas & Margrett was borne The 15th day of ye 2d moth in ye yeare 1679.

10 Joshua: Jordan sonn of ye afore sd Thomas & Margrett was borne The last day of ye 6th month in ye yeare: 1681.

Thomas Jordan of Chuckatuck in Nanzemond County in Virginia was Born in ye year 1634 and in ye year 1660 hee Received ye truth and A Bode faithfull in it: and in Constant unity wth ye faithfull frends there of: and stood in opposision Against all wrong & Desatefull spiritts: haveing suffered ye spoiling of his goods: & ye Imprisonment of his Body for ye truth sake: and Continued in ye truth unto the End of his dayes: is ye Beleefe—of us his Dear wife & Children above Ritten   Hee Departed this Life ye Eight day of ye tenth month on ye sixth day of ye weeke about ye second hour in ye afternoone and was Buryed ye twelfe day of ye said month on ye third day of ye weeke in ye year 1699.

[Sarah Jordan great Grandchild of ye above mentioned worthy Elder Tho Jordan & Daughter of Jos & Anne Jordan was born ye 12th day of ye 2 mo 1731.

Abigail Jordan Daughter of the said Joseph & Anne Jordan was Born ye 14th day of ye 7th mo 1733.

Margarett Jordan third and last Daughter of ye sd Joseph & Anne * * * * * * * *]¶

¶ The above entries in brackets have been crossed out in the original, but are still legible, so far as given above. These entries will also be found later on.

formerly   Tho: Page & Alce his wife their childrens
of
Nanzemund   Nativitties Recorded as followeth:
County

Tho: Page ye son of ye Afore sd Thomas & Alce was borne ye Seventh day of ye 2d month in ye year: 1680.—

Rebecka daughter of ye aforesd Thomas & Alce was borne the Eaight of ye Eleventh in ye year: 1682—

of Islaweight   Henry wiggs & Katherens his first & second
County   wifes ther Childrens Nativitties recorded

Henry wiggs ye son of the afore sd Henry & Kathren his first wife was borne the sixt day of ye Eleventh month 1675.

Kathren wiggs ye daughter of ye afore sd Henry & Kathrern his second wife was borne ye second day of ye 8 month 1681.

Mary wiggs ye daughter of ye above sd Henry & Katheren his second wife was borne: ye second month: 1687

Elizabeth wiggs ye daughter of ye above sd Henry & Kathren his second wife was borne ye 16th day of ye 12th month 1689.

Sara wiggs the daughter of the afore sd Henry & Kathren was borne 19 day 12: mo 169—[2?]

William wiggs sonn of ye afore sd Henry & Katheren was borne ye Last of ye 5th moth 1696

John Harris & his wife Margret of ye county of Isleaweight there Childrens Nativitties Recorded as followeth—

1 Margarett Harris ye daughter of ye afore sd John & Margret was borne the thirteenth day of ye: 6: moth: in ye year: 1682

2 Allis: Harris ye daughter of the afore sd John & Margret was borne the seventh day of ye: 6th month in ye yeare 1685

Margret Harris wife of ye afore sd John died ye 16 of ye 11 moth 1687

3 Elizabeth Harris ye daughter of ye afore sd John & Elizabeth his second wife was borne ye: 15th of ye 3d month —1692

4 Isabella Harris daughter of ye afore sd John & Elizabeth was born the seventh day of ye forth month in ye year 1695

5 Sasanna Harris daughter of the above sd John Elizabeth was Born the 19 day of the 11 Mo in year 1699.

6 Anne Harris Daughter of the sd Jn° & Elizabeth was Born on the 18 day of the 11 mo in the year 1702

7 Mary Harris Daughter to the above sd Jn° & Elizabeth was Born on the 12 day of the 3 mo Called may in the year 1706.

Thomas Jordan ye younger and his wife Elizabeth There childrens Nativitties Recorded in Chuckatuck as followeth

Thomas Jordan ye sonn of Thomas & Elizabeth aforesd was borne y Nineteenth day of ye fift month in ye year; 1681.

Elizabeth Jordan the daughter of ye afore sd was borne ye Eaighteenth day of ye Ninthe: 9 month calld November— 1683

Martha Jordan was borne ye daughter of ye afore sd on ye twenty second of ye Eleventh month January—1685

William Jordan ye sonn of ye afore sd Thomas & Elizabeth was borne the 25th day of ye: 5th month in ye year: 1688.

William Scott and Elizabeth his wife their Childrens nativities Recorded

Elizabeth Scott daughter of the above sd wm & Elizabeth was born on the 12 day of Decembr in the year 1675:....

Wm Scott son to the above sd Wm & Elizabeth was born on the 27 of decembr in the year 1678

John Scot was Born on the 3 day of the second mo in the year 1682

Robt Scot was Born on the 19 day of the 4 mo Called June in the year 1685.

Sarah Scot was Born on the 5 day of the 5 mo in the yeare 1694

Kathren Scot was Born on the 9 day of the 4 mo In the year 1697

John Scott & his wife Elizabeth there Childrens Nativities Recorded as folloeth

william Scott ye sonn of ye Above sd John & Elizabeth was borne ye: 8th day of ye 3 moth: 1683

Elizabeth ye daughter of ye sd Jo^n & Eliz. was borne ye 5th day of ye 2 mon in ye yer: 1686.

Edmond Belson & his wife Mary ther Childrens Nativities Recorded as folloeth

Mary the daughter of ye afore sd Edmond & Mary was borne: ye 24 day of ye Eleventh month: 1685

Elizabeth ye daughter of ye afore sd was borne ye: 13th day of ye: 11 moth 1687

Beniamin Small & Elizabeth his wife their Children Births Recorded

Amy Small Daughter to the above sd Beniamin & Elizabeth was Born on the 30 day of the first mo 1702

Hannah Small Daughter to the above sd Beniamin & Elizabeth Small was Born upon the last day of the third mo in the year 1704

John Morry & Elizabeth yarrat daughter of William yarrat of the Ille white County did propound theire marriage before a meeting of frends: and coming before the meeting the second time did publish their mariage againe and were married before an appointed meeting of Friends in the howse of Wm Yarratt hir father on this twenty second day of ye 6 month in ye year: 1678

John Murry
Elizabeth Yarratt

Witnesses:

William: Yarratt:	Mathew Wakle
John Graue:	Edward Mathews
Robart Willson:	Tho: Jordan
Edward Perkins:	Wᵐ Oudelant
william Pope:	Margret Tabbarer
Henry wiggs:—	Margret Jordan
william Boody	Susana Bressie
John Walton:	Mary Tooke
Thomas Tooke	Anna Boody
Giles Limscott	Julian Wakly
John Coker	Wm Poope Junʳ
Arther: Jones	Henry Poope
frances Wren	Tho: Jordan Junʳ

William Oudelant of Chucatucke in ye county of Nanze-mund: And Christian Taberer the daughter of: Thomas: Taberer of the county of Islle a weight did propound theire marriage before a meeting of frends at Thomas Jordans house in Chucatuck ye 14 day of ye 7 month last: and coming before ye meeting ye second time at Wᵐ Yarrats at Pagan Creeke did publish their mariage againe one the 7 day of the: 9: month after: And were married in a meeting apoynted for yᵗ purpose in yᵉ house of Elizabeth Oudelants his mother on this fifteenth day of yᵉ: 9: month In yᵉ yeare: 1678.

> William: Oudelant
> Christian Taberer

Witnesses:

Thomas: Taberer	Thomas Tooke
Margaret: Taberer	John Morry
Elizabeth Oudelant	Thomas Scuthins
William: Yarrat	James Hill
Thomas: Jordan	Susana Bresei
	Mary Tooke

Richard: Ratlyfe

John: Cop^eland

Joseph: Cop^eland

Edmond: Belson

William Pope

Henry: Wiggs

Margaret: Jordan

Thomas wombwell

Henry Pope and

2 Justices of ye peace viz:

Barnabe Keaone

& Tho: Godwin

EARLY QUAKER RECORDS IN VIRGINIA.

Daniel Sanboarn on 9 day of 11 mo. 1706 gave his consent to the meeting for Joseph Woodson to marry his daughter Mary.

John Scot on 10 of 3 mo. 1707 sent an acknowledgment for his error in marrying Joan Took in the manner he did; he thought she was a member of Pagon Creek meeting.

Daniel Akehurst Departed this Life the Eight day of the 11 m° in the year 1699

Richd Rickesis Departed this life on the 29 day of the 7 m° in the year 1703 about the tenth hour in the morning.

Elizabeth Small Daughter of Edmond Belson & mary Belson of nansemond County Departed this Life the 25th day of ye 7th mon in the year 1717.

Catherin Ricks Departed this Life ye 1th Day of ye 8th mon in ye year 1717

Wm Scott ye elder Departed this Life ye 11th Day of ye 8th mon in ye year 1717.

Isaack Ricks Depared this Life ye 3^d day of 11th: mo^th 1723

Richard Jordan Departed this Life ye 29th of 10th mo: 1723.

[Three fourths of a page cut out.]

Katheren wiggs Departed this life the twelfe day of the Eleaventh month 1675.

the Buriall of jeams Hill:

Rachill Hill Buried the tenth day of the first month *1674*

Josife Hill Buried the fourteenth day the second month 1674

Elizabeth Hill the wife of jeams Hill Buried the 16th day of the 3^d month 1674

An: Hill Buried the 16th day of the 8 month *1674*

Hannah Outland the wife of Cornelius Outland departed this life the Eleaventh day of the first month *1676*

William Denson ye Elder departed this Life ye Eaight day of ye first month: 1676.

Cornelius Oudeland: departed this Life on y^e: 13th day of the 12mo: 1676

william Galliway of Scotland A minester of ye Gospell of Jesus Christ departed this Life on ye 27th of the 5 moth 1677

Mary Copland wife of Joseph Copland departed this Life ye 27th day of the: 3 month: 1678.

William Yarrat ye younger departed this Life towards ye latter Eand of ye yeare in: 1676

Margaret yarrat wife of william yarret the Elder and mother of the younger departed this Life abought a year after in 1677.

Edmond Bellson departed this life the 19 day of the 1 month in the year 1679

Ruth Harris ye daughter of John Harris died y^e: 11th of ye 4th m^o *1679*

William yarrat the Elder departed this Life y^e ————

william outeland departed this Life ye 24 day of ye 5 moth in ye yeare 1687

Thomas Hollowell ye Elder died ye 16 of ye 1 moth 1687

Edmond Hollowell his son died ye 15 day of ye 2 moth 1687

Mary Belson ye wif of Edmond Belson of Nanzemund departed this Life The: 18th day of y^e: 12: month: 1687

Christian Jordan the wife of Robart Jordan departed this Life ye 26 of ye 6 ^{mo} 1689

Tho. Hollowell ye Elder departed this Life ye 16 of ye first moth 1687*

Edmond Hollowell yᵉ son of yᵉ aforesd Thomas Hollowell of Elizabeth River died yᵉ 15 of 2ᵈ moᵗʰ after.*

Wᵐ Rickesis the son of Isaac Rickesis departed this life the 22 day of the sixth m° Aboate halfe and houre before the goeing down of the sun In the year 1694: hee being almost 24 years of age.

Alice Hollowell widdow of Thomas Hollowell deceased the Elder Departed this Life this 19 day of the 9 m° in the yeare 1700

Jacob Rickesis the sonn of Isaac Rickesis & Kathren his wife departed this Life upon the † day of the fivfth m° about the first hour in the Afternoon

Thomas Page Junor his sonˢ Birth Recorded & daughter

first Thomas Page the son of Thomas Page & Isabell his wife was Born on the 7 day of the Tenth m° in the: year 1703 (?)

2 Elizabeth Page daughter to the aboveˢᵈ Thomas & Isabell his wife was born on the 30 day of the 4 m° In the year 1706

3: Henry Page sonn to the Abovesᵈ Thomas Page and Isabell his wife was Born on the ninth day of the second m° in the year 1708-9

Abraham Rickes and Mary his wife their childrens nativities Recorded

Mary Rickes Daughter to the aboveˢᵈ Abraham & Mary was Born on the first day of the 7 m° in the year 1704.

Elizabeth Rickes Daughter to the aboveˢᵈ Abraham & Mary was born on the 18 day of the 11 m° In the year 1706.

Isaac Rickes Junor and Sarah his wife their Childrens nativities Recorded

Wᵐ Rickes son of the Abovesᵈ Isaac & Sarah his wife was Born on the 25 day of the 7 m° In the year 1698.

---

* These two entries have been crossed off, being a duplicate of entries above.

† The words fifth and ninth have both been crossed out leaving the day of the month uncertain.

Isaac Rickes son of the above^sd Isaac & Sarah was Born on the 27 of the 12 m° in the year 1702

Jacob Rickes sonn to the Above^sd Isaac & Sarah was Born on the 11 day of the second m° In the year 1705

[Several pages cut out. Then follow letters from Joseph Glaister and from various meetings in England.]

Att A mans meeting att Chuckatuck in the County of nanzemond held the 9 of the 8 m° 1707

That wereas some friends being Disattisfied as concer nathan newby^s testimony Complaint Being made to ye monthly meeting Before this the meeting was Pleased to Defere itt to this meeting above mentioned for A further Consideration & a Careful enquiry being made as Concer the matter the meeting was Pleased in order to Proceed to Putt & end to this difference some friends being Appoynted for that Purpose & did Proceed in order their unto according to the best of their Judg^mt & wee the subscribers doe give our sence & Jud^mt Concerning our friend nathan newby that hee is a man that feares the Lord and that his Call is to the ministry and that itt is of God and that hee has A share with the Rest of his Brethren in the ministry & that it is our sence & Judg^mt that hee ought not to bee made & offender for the word or the like & tho some doe say that they doe not Receive Refresment from his ministry others say they have Received Refresment from his—through his ministry & hee allwaies Appeared to us the subscribers to bee willing to spend & to bee spent for the honnor & Glory of God And wee dare not disencourage him in his testimony but desieres that the Lord may Prosper him and bee with him to the end of his daies desiering that hee may be Carefull neither to outgoe his Gide nor linger behind him sence hee that makes hast may miss his way And hee that stayes behind lose his Gide and this is our sence & Judgment And if any amongst us friend or friends should Aproach unto the Lord in prayer and if any Amongst us Profesing Truth with should att any time sitt with their hatts on in the time of

Prayer unsattisfied with the friend so concerned that they ought to be brought to Jud^mt except the friend is denied by a meeting of friends

Isaac Rickes	Daniell Sanbourn
Jn° Small	Richard Rattliff
Sarah Sanbourn	John Porter

Levied By Distress of Jn° simons for the year 1704: 48 poundes of Tobb itt being for his Parrish levy.

Levied by distress of Jn° simins for the year: 1706: 18 lb of Tobb itt being for his parish Levy.

Levied by distress for the year 1707: 98 poundes of Tobb itt being for his parish levy.

I say Recd pr Jn° King Church warden for the Branch parish

Sesed for ministers dewes & Clerkes dewes a hundred poundes of this with Receipts

By mee John King Church warden.

"Margarett Jordan the Daughter of Robt Brashare was Born in the seventh m° in the year 1642 and was Convinced of the Truth about the 16 year of her Age from wch time shee lived and exemplary life in all Conversation untill the day of her death and was a sufferer with my father both by Confinemen^t and alsoe the spoyling of their Goods by the Adversaries of Truth for the exercise of their Concience in the worship of God whose whose hearts was Given up in the service of Truth according to her Ability. shee was A Good wife A tender And A Carefull mother A Good mistris And a kind neighbour And Aboute the 63 year of her Age shee was Taken with and Indisposition of Boddy wch Contanued near 3 years in wch time shee was much weakened by Reason of her distemper & A little before her death some friends Come to see her to whome shee signified her Content & spake much to them of the Goodness of God to her & s^d shee Questioned not of her salvation & upon A first day of the weeke being the fifth of the m° shee spoke to mee

& s^d that there was A Time for her to die & that was her Time & Itt was Come. And on the Third day of the weeke as I was standing by her to see her last end shee Called mee by my name And s^d I am Gone. I Answered & s^d I thought shee would Goe to God, shee Answered with A Chearfull & a smilling Countenance I doe not doubt that And s^d Rememb^r my love to All friends & unto my Children And tell them that they fear god And love one Another And keep to meetings And then itt will bee well with them And bad mee send for my Eldest Brothers wife to whome when shee Came and severall of my Brothers shee s^d to them that they weare Come now to see her Last End And att 6 of the clock att night shee died in Remarkable Quietness the 7 day of the 10 m^o in the year 1708 haveing Lived About 66 years And survived my father 9 yeares lacking eighteen houres And was Buried the 11 day of the afores^d m^o

Ben^n Jordan Testimony Concer his Mothre.

Heare follows And Adition by Joseph Glaister

Iff the Righteous bee had in Everlasting Remembrance And thot noe man shutt A Door In the house of the Lord nor Kindle a fire upon his Altar in vain nor Give A Cup of Cold water to A disciple of X^t In the name of A Disciple butt shall have a Plentifull Reward att the hand of the Pure Rightious Liveing Eternall God how then shall they Bee wrapt up in Eternall Joy And Consolation as the Recompence of the Just that hath served the Lord with their All opening their doores & heartes to faithful messengers & living minesters of our Lord And Saviour Jesus X^t doeing what they doe as unto God & not unto Man knowing that of him they have their Reward amongst the number of those servants of the Lord And Church of X^t was our well Esteemed and serviceable friend Margaret Jordan deceased one whoe fullfilled that saying Cast your Bread upon the waters for After Many daies you shall find Itt noe Question of her Reaping of the fruits of her Labours haveing her mind steadfastly Bent to doe good in her day shee Continued In Great service unto the Church untill her last In this Low woreld And being Taken from her service hear as well as from All trouble that did or might Attend her Earthly Pilgrimage shee is Entred Into that Rest & Peace that Time will never wear out but weare shee will have a Plentifull & A Peaceable Reward & as Itt was Comended to the Church as vertues X^t of God Comanding to minester to the saints to wash their feet And dillegently to follow every Good worke wch service I doe desire may bee studied By All that In the Eyes of God will bee more Esteemed & Render men more happy as they dilligently follow every Good work then all woreldly Honnours Can Render them

Nanzemond the 29 of the 3 mo 1709

Joseph Glaister"

[Most of a page cut out. The entries of births of five persons of Nansemond having been thereon.]

Seesed of Joshua Jordan for Preists tiths as followeth seised January ye 29th of m^r Joshua Jordan ninety pounds of Tobbo for the minnisters Dues for ye year 1717 by George Narsworthy Sheriff.

Seised Jany the 29th 1717 by vertue of an Execution bareing date y^e 22th Day of may 1715 of m^r Joshua Jordan two hundred fourty six and my fees twenty pounds of Tobb^{co} it being for minnisters Dues upon account of Andrew Woodley by me   George Narsworthy Shr.

(Concluded.)

INDEX

INDEX

Glaister, Joseph 1, 51, 53, 54
Godwin, Edmond 9
  Elizabeth 7, 8, 9
  Thomas 7, 8, 9, 26, 47
Good, John 14
Goodman, Rebecka 4
  William 3
Granberry, John 13
Granbery, William 6
Graue, John 11, 46
Greefes, Peeter 11
  Sara 11
Green, Geo. 26
  Jno. 20
Greeves, Peter 14

-H-

Hackly/Hacly/Hackley
  Ann 10, 12
  Henry 7, 8, 11, 12, 17
Haile, Mary 28
Hall, Eliz. 4
  Felicia 33
  Henry 4
  Moses 5, 33
Hallowell (see Hollowell)
Hampton, Elizabeth 24
  Thos. 30
Hancock, Will. 3
Hancoke, Eliz. 4
Hanell, (Capt.) 26
Harris, Allis 43
  Anne 44
  Elizabeth 22, 44
  Isabella 44
  John 11, 14, 15, 22, 43, 44,
   49
  Margarett/Margret 43
  Mary 44
  Ruth 49
  Sasanna 44
  Tho. 11
Harrison, John 22
  Willm./Wm. 22, 31
Hill, An. 49
  Elizabeth 49
  James 46
  Jeams 48, 49
  Josife 48
  Rachill 48

Hodges, Mary 7
  Tho. 5, 12
Hollowell, Alce/Allice/Allis/
  Alic/Alice/Alise 3, 4, 6, 10,
   11, 12, 17, 36, 37, 50
  Beniamine 36
  Edmond 36, 49, 50
  Elizabeth 6, 12, 15, 16, 20,
   36, 37
  Henry 10, 11, 12, 20, 36
  Jno. 5
  John 12, 36, 37
  Joseph 6, 12, 36
  Sarah 36
  Thomas 3, 4, 6, 35, 36, 37, 49,
   50
Hooles, Barbery 3
Hopkins, Ricd. 5
Horning, Robt. 29
  Sarah 19, 24
Howard, Sarah 12
Hutchins, Francis 23, 30

-I-

Iles, Jno. 25

-J-

Johnstone, James 3
Jones, Arther 46
  Martha 10, 12
  Robart/Robard 4, 10, 12, 17
  Robt. 6, 7, 8, 12
  Sara 14
Jordan, Abigail 42
  Anne 42
  Beniamin(e)/Benjamine 16, 18,
   27, 28, 42
  Benn. 53
  Christian 7, 8, 9, 28, 49
  Dorrithy 18
  Elis 34
  Elizabeth 6, 7, 8, 9, 10, 18,
   29, 31, 32, 44
  James 8, 9, 10, 13, 15, 16, 17,
   18, 20, 26, 27, 29, 31, 32,
   41
  James Sr. 9, 10

62

Woodson, Joseph 48
Woory, Elizabeth 7, 8
　Joseph 9
Wren, Frances 46
Wright, John 35
　Mary 32, 35

-Y-

Yarrat (see Yarrett)
Yarratt (see Yarrett)
Yarrett/Yarratt
　Elizabeth 37, 45
　Katheren 37, 38
　Margaret/Margrett 37, 49
　William 37, 45, 46, 49
Yearly, William 16